WS

755

Colours We Eat

Blue and Purple Foods

Isabel Thomas

www.raintreepublishers.co.uk
Visit our website to find out more information about **Raintree** books.

To order:
☎ Phone 44 (0) 1865 888112
📄 Send a fax to 44 (0) 1865 314091
🖥 Visit the Raintree Bookshop at **www.raintreepublishers.co.uk** to browse our catalogue and order online.

First published in Great Britain by Raintree,
Halley Court, Jordan Hill, Oxford OX2 8EJ,
part of Harcourt Education.
Raintree is a registered trademark of Harcourt
Education Ltd.

Editorial: Richard Woodham
Design: Richard Parker
Picture Research: Ruth Blair
Production: Kevin Blackman

Originated by Dot Gradations
Printed and bound in China by South China
Printing Company

ISBN 1 844 21446 X
08 07 06 05 04
10 9 8 7 6 5 4 3 2 1

British Library Cataloguing in Publication Data
Thomas, Isabel
Blue and Purple Foods
641.3
A full catalogue record for this book is available
from the British Library.

Acknowledgements
The publishers would like to thank the following
for permission to reproduce photographs:
Anthony Blake Photo Library pp. 15 (Karen
Thomas), 17 (John Carey), 19 (Eaglemoss Consumer
Publications); Food Features p. 9; Heinemann
Library pp. 4, 5, 6, 7, 8, 12, 13, 14, 16, 17, 18,
20, 21, 21 (Tudor Photography); Holt Studios p. 16
(Nigel Cattlin).

Cover photograph of a spread of blue and purple
foods reproduced with permission of Heinemann
Library (Tudor Photography).

Every effort has been made to contact copyright
holders of any material reproduced in this book.
Any omissions will be rectified in subsequent
printings if notice is given to the publishers.

❗ CAUTION: Children should be supervised by an adult when preparing food and using kitchen utensils.

Some words are shown in bold, **like this.** You can find them in the glossary on page 23.

Contents

Have you eaten blue or purple foods? . . 4

Which fruits are blue or purple? 6

Which vegetables are blue or purple? . . 8

Which blue or purple foods are soft? . . 10

Which foods have purple skin? 12

Have you tried these strange blue
  or purple foods? 14

Have you tried these other blue or
  purple foods? 16

Which liquids are purple? 18

Recipe: Blueberry cream cheese spread . 20

Quiz 22

Glossary 23

Index. 24

Have you eaten blue or purple foods?

Colours are all around us.

How many different colours can you see in this picture?

All of these foods are blue
or purple.

Have you eaten any of them?

Which fruits are blue or purple?

Blueberries are small and round. They are often used in cooking.

Have you ever eaten a blueberry muffin?

stone

Plums grow on trees.

They have hard **seeds** inside them, called stones.

7

Which vegetables are blue or purple?

Some broccoli has purple flowers.

Broccoli is good for you.

Did you know that some carrots are purple?

They are orange inside!

Which blue or purple foods are soft?

The blue bits in this cheese are a kind of **mould** that you can eat.

Blue cheese is very smelly!

Aubergines are vegetables with smooth, shiny skin.

They are white and soft inside.

Which foods have purple skin?

Figs have hard, purple skin.

They are soft and pink inside.

seed

skin

These are passion fruits.

When their skin goes wrinkly, the fruit inside is **ripe** and ready to eat.

Have you tried these strange blue or purple foods?

This vegetable is called a blue kohlrabi.

We can eat the stem and the leaves.

These blue potatoes look
very strange.

They taste just like
normal potatoes.

Have you tried these other blue or purple foods?

This vegetable is called a red cabbage.

But it is actually purple!

Purple basil is a **herb**.

People use herbs to add **flavour** to food.

Which liquids are purple?

This is purple grape juice.

It is made by squeezing the juice out of black grapes.

This is a blueberry smoothie.

It is made by mixing blueberries with milk.

Recipe: Blueberry cream cheese spread

❶ Ask an adult to help you.

First, mash blueberries into some cream cheese until it turns purple.

Sprinkle on a spoon of sugar and mash that in, too.

Now spread your blueberry cream cheese on to some bread or a bagel.

Yum!

Quiz

Can you remember what these blue and purple foods are called?

Look for the answers on page 24.

Glossary

flavour
what something tastes like

herb
plant that has a strong taste and is used in cooking

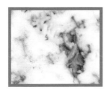
mould
sort of fungus

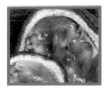
ripe
soft and ready to eat

seeds
parts of a plant that can grow into new plants

Index

aubergines   11

blueberry   6, 19, 20, 21

broccoli   8

cabbage   16

carrot   9

cheese   10

cream cheese   20, 21

figs   12

grape   18

herb   17

kohlrabi   14

mould   10

passion fruit   13

plums   7

potato   15

purple basil   17

seeds   7, 13

Answers to quiz on page 22

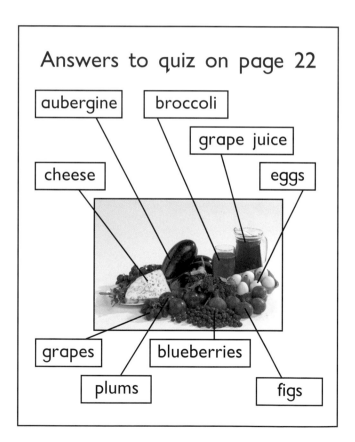

aubergine

broccoli

grape juice

cheese

eggs

grapes

blueberries

plums

figs

24

Titles in the Colours We Eat series include:

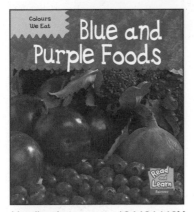

Hardback   184421446X

Hardback   1844214451

Hardback   1844214486

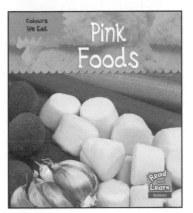

Hardback   1844214494

Hardback   1844214478

Find out about the other titles in this series on our website www.raintreepublishers.co.uk